Netherland
Coloring The World

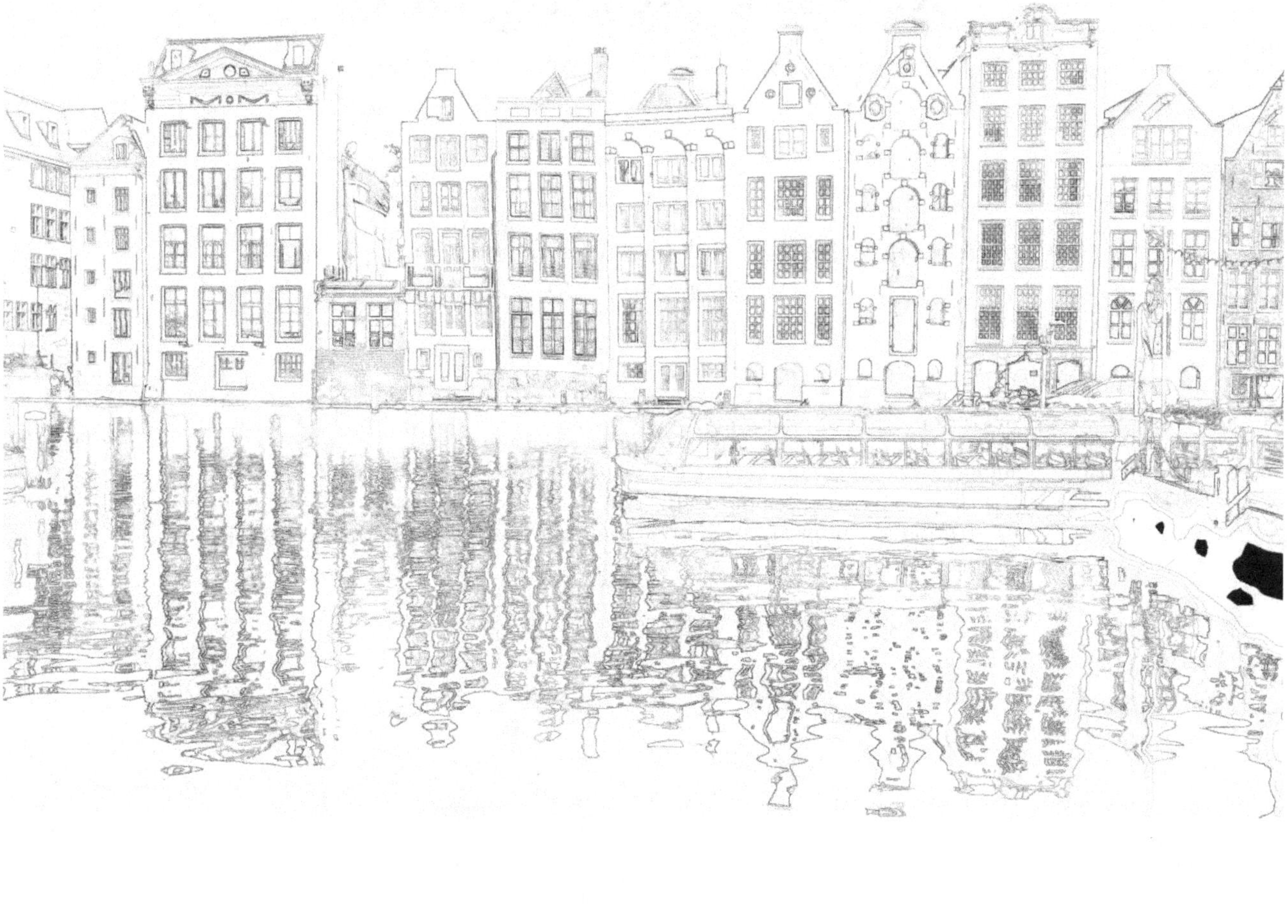

Anthony Hutzler

Sketch Coloring Book

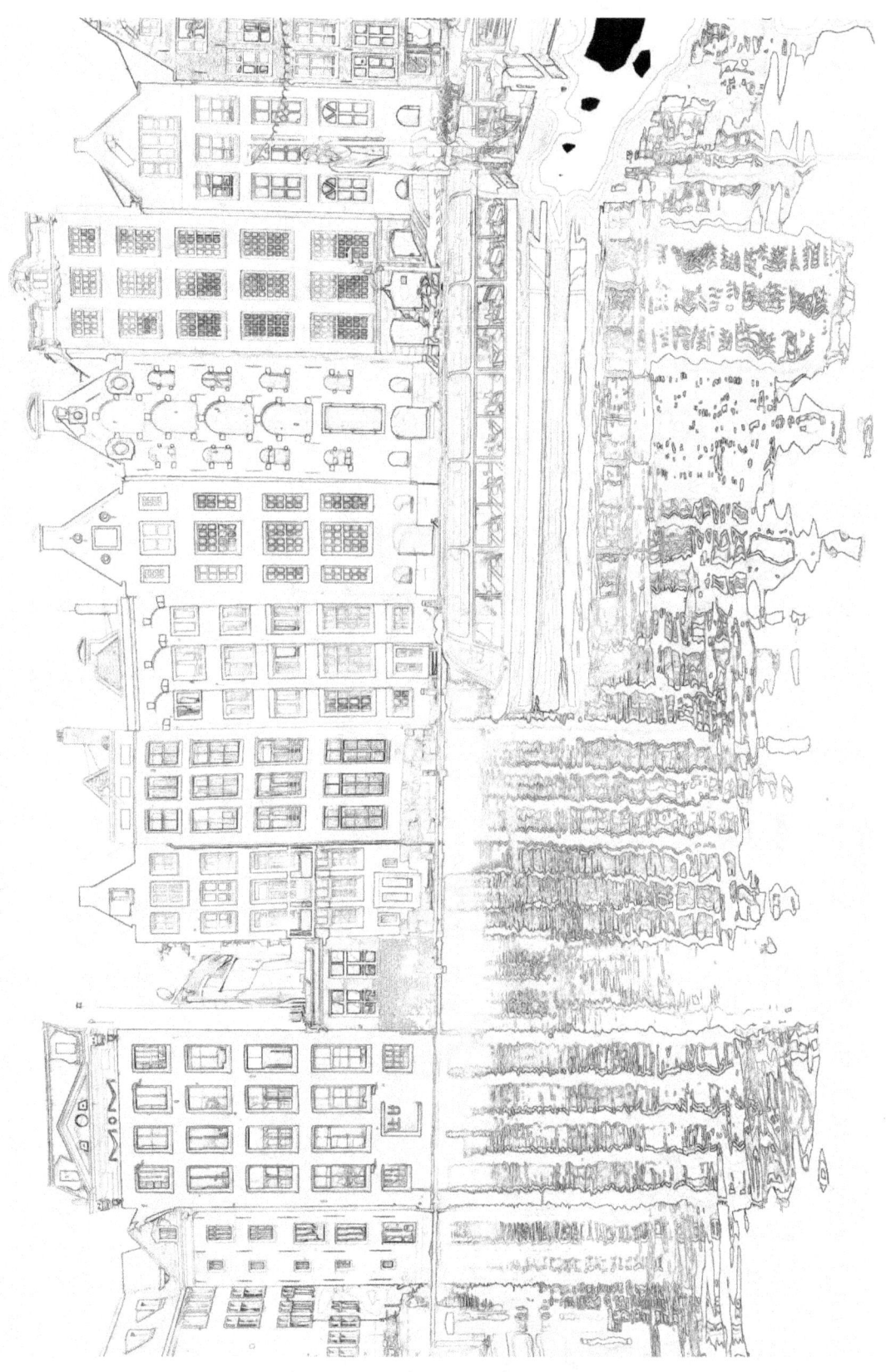

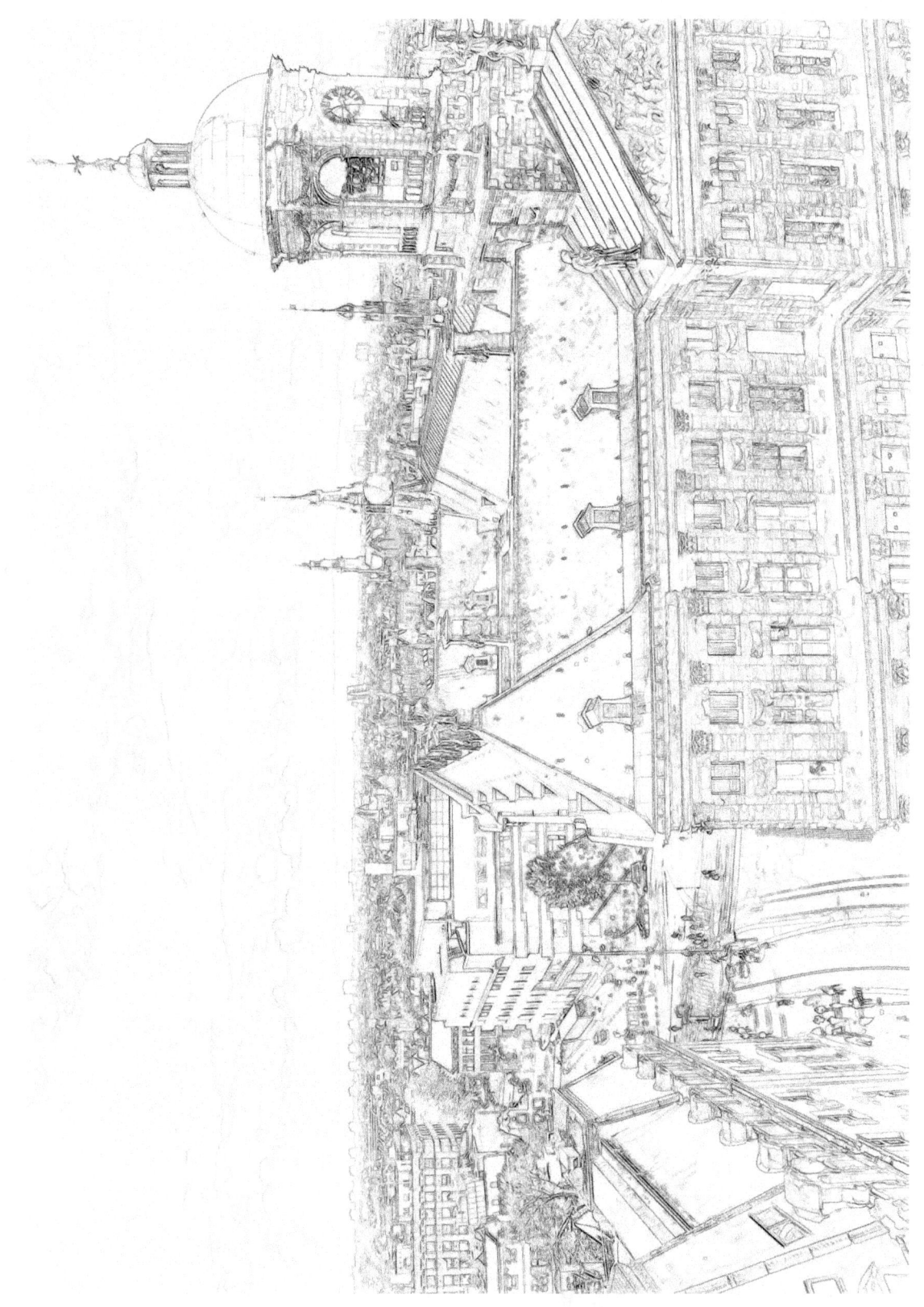

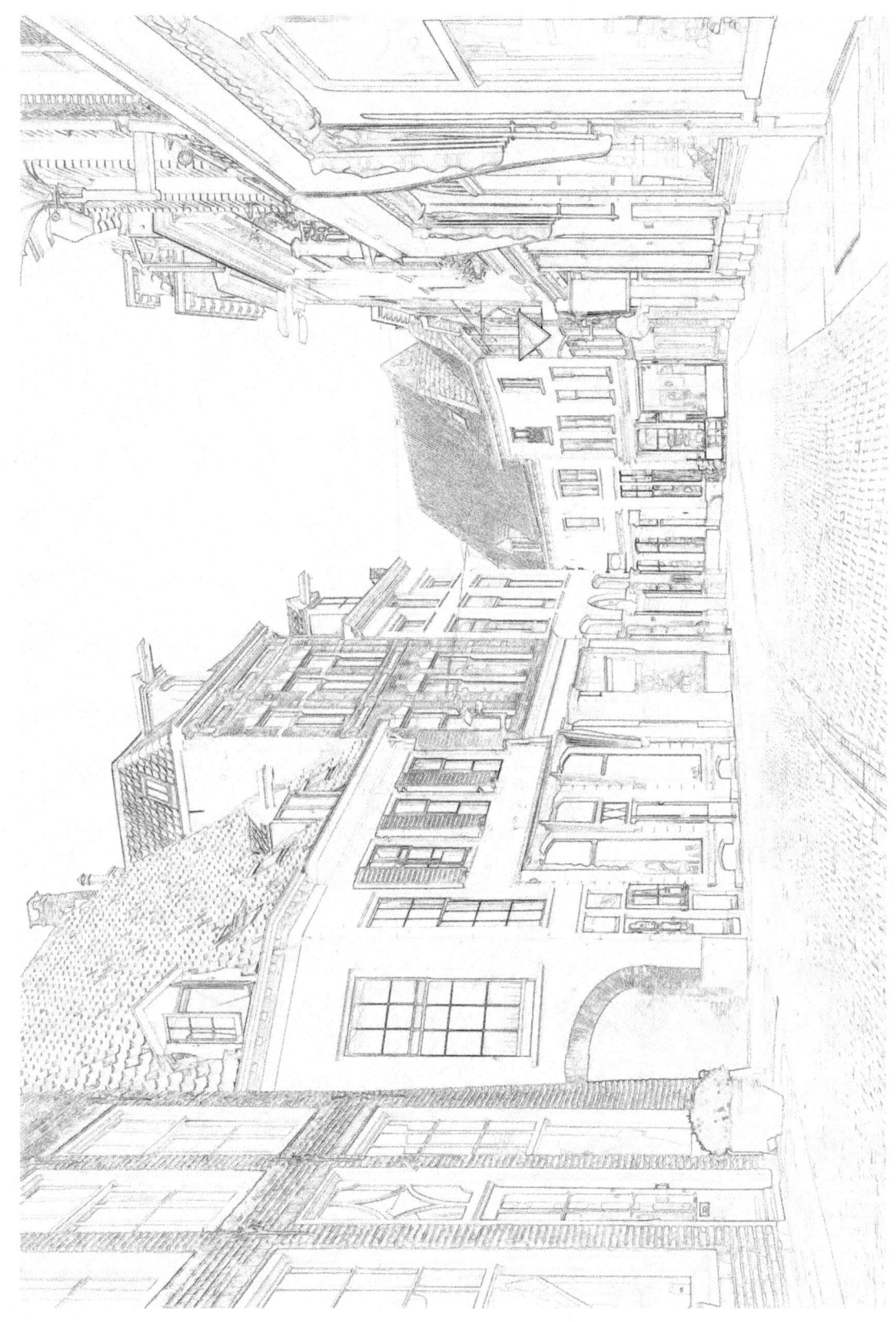

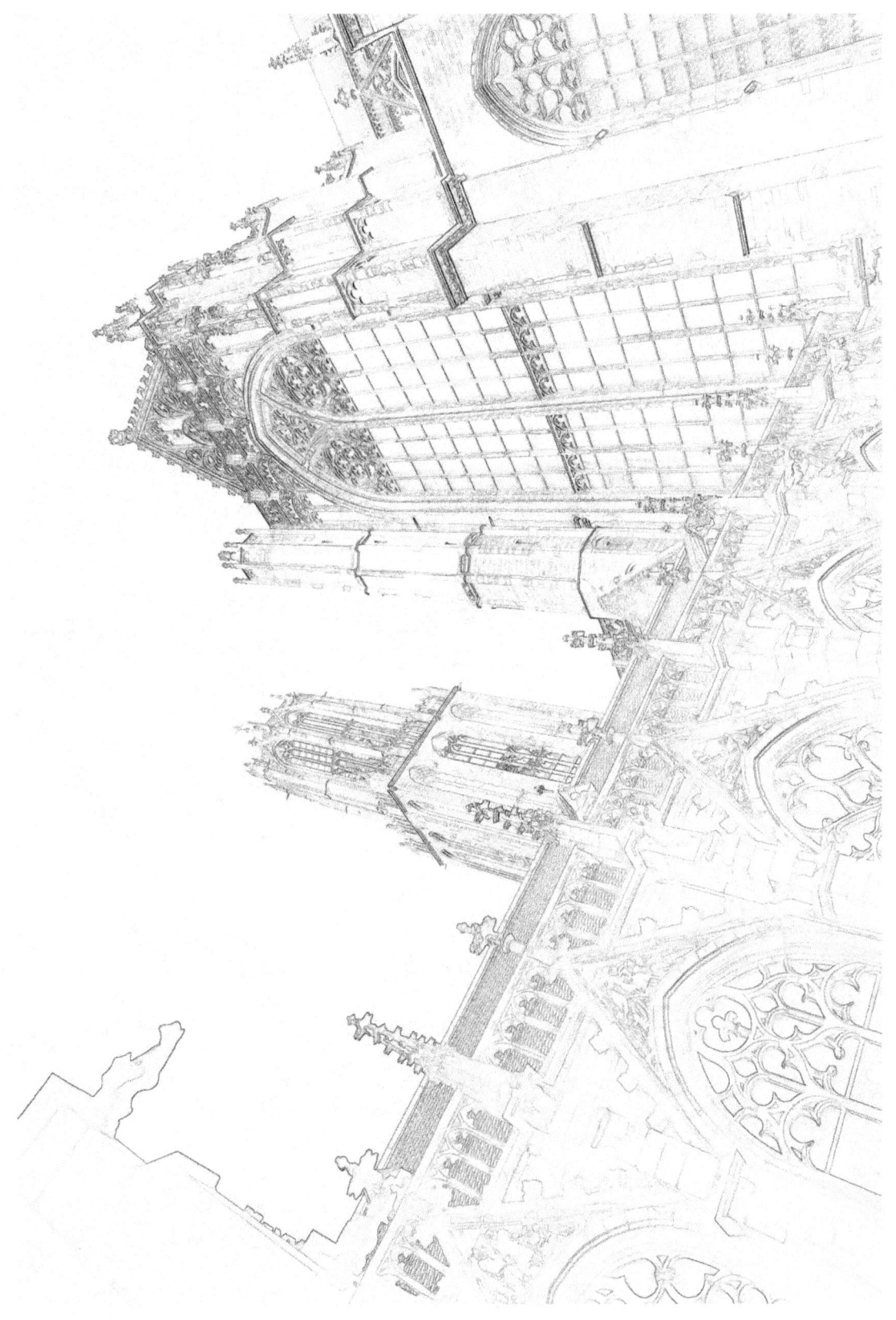

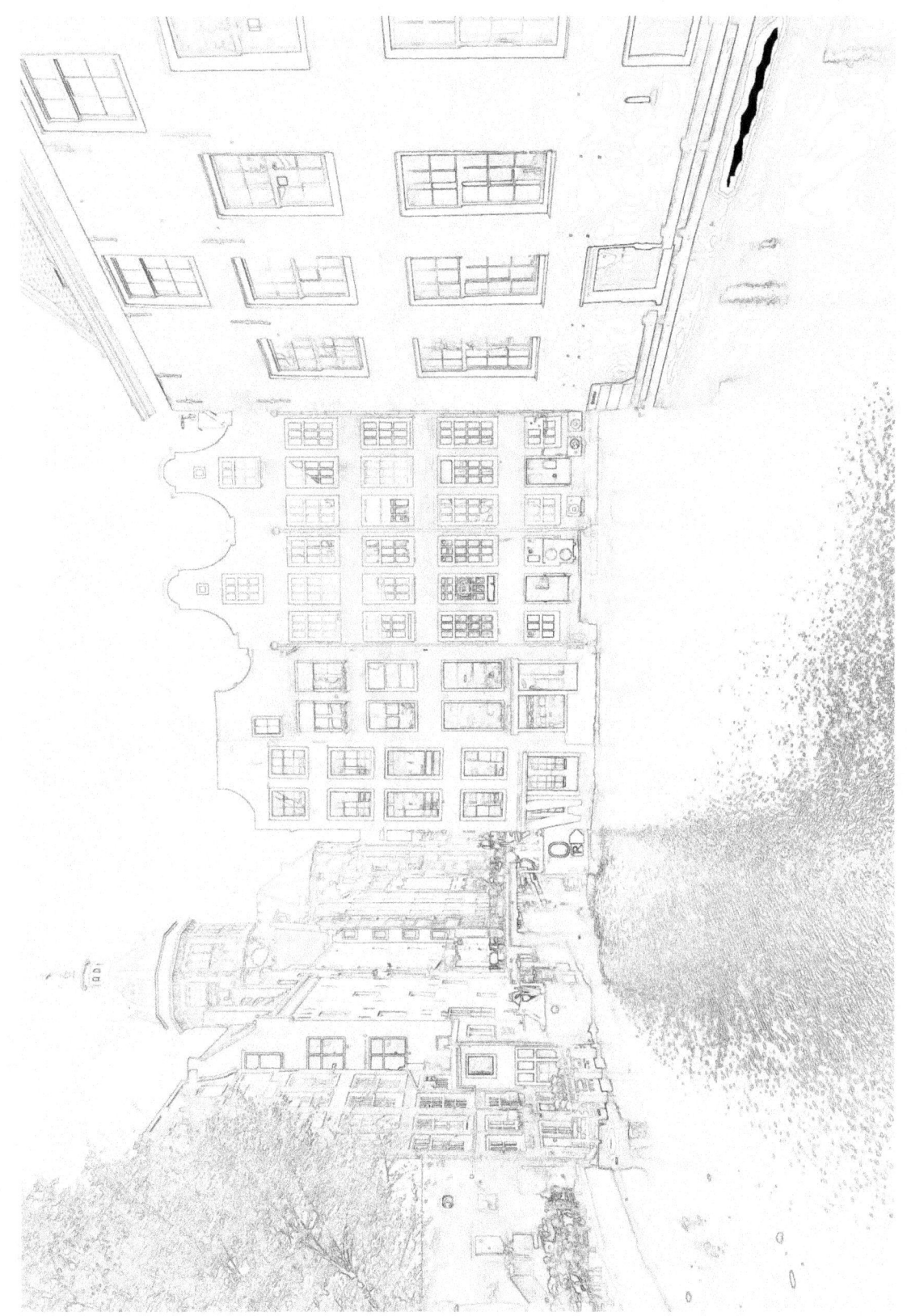

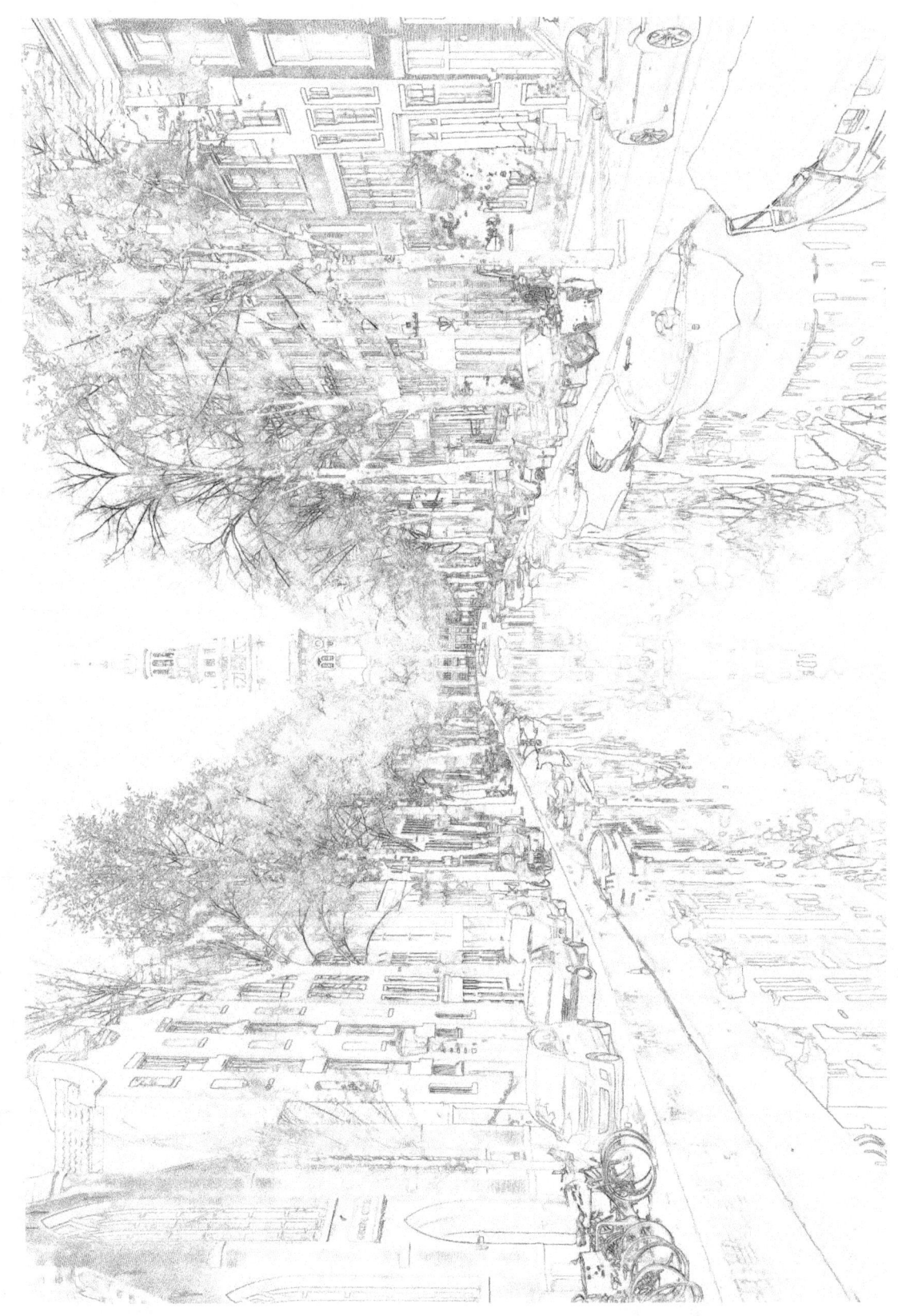

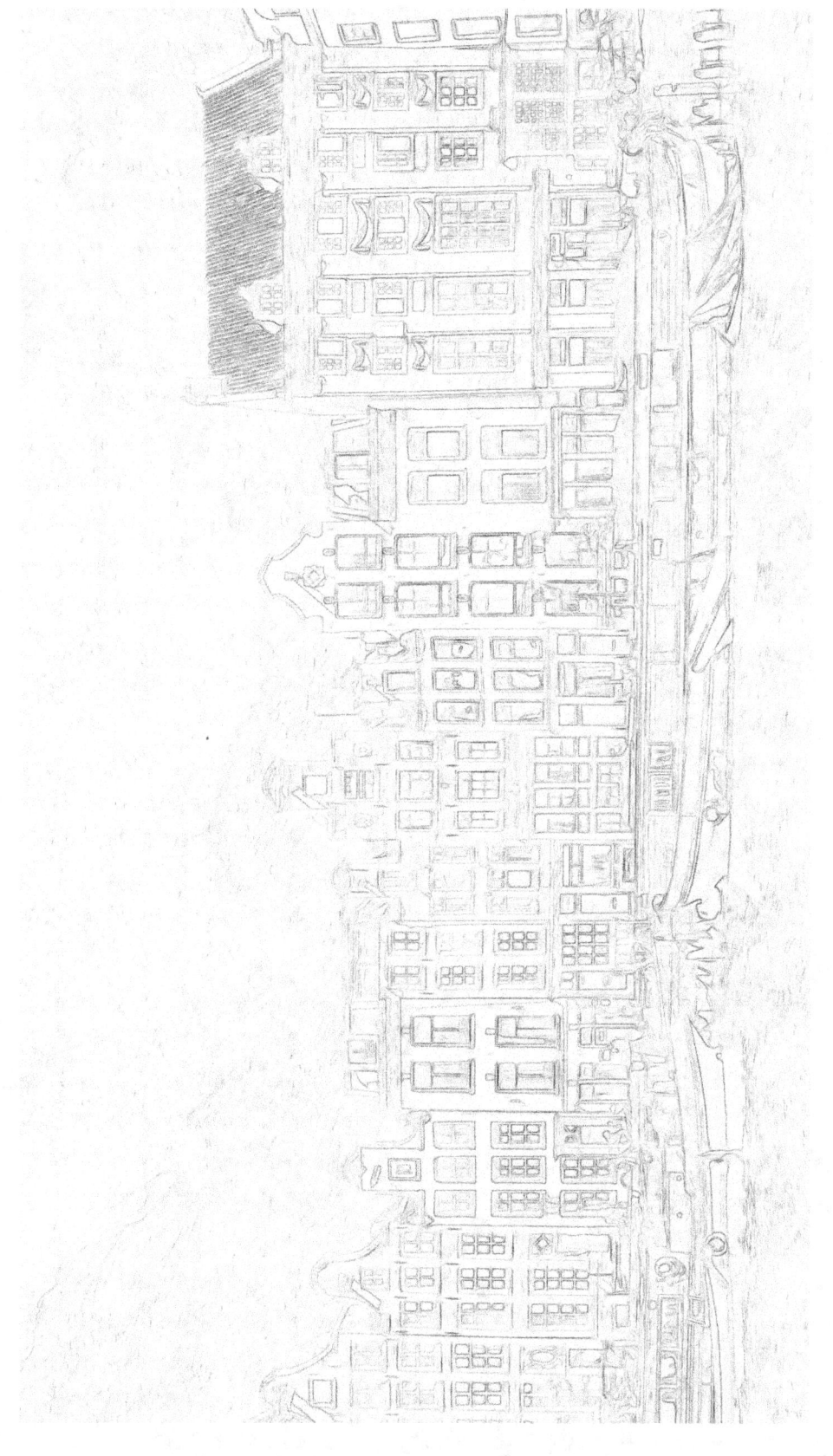

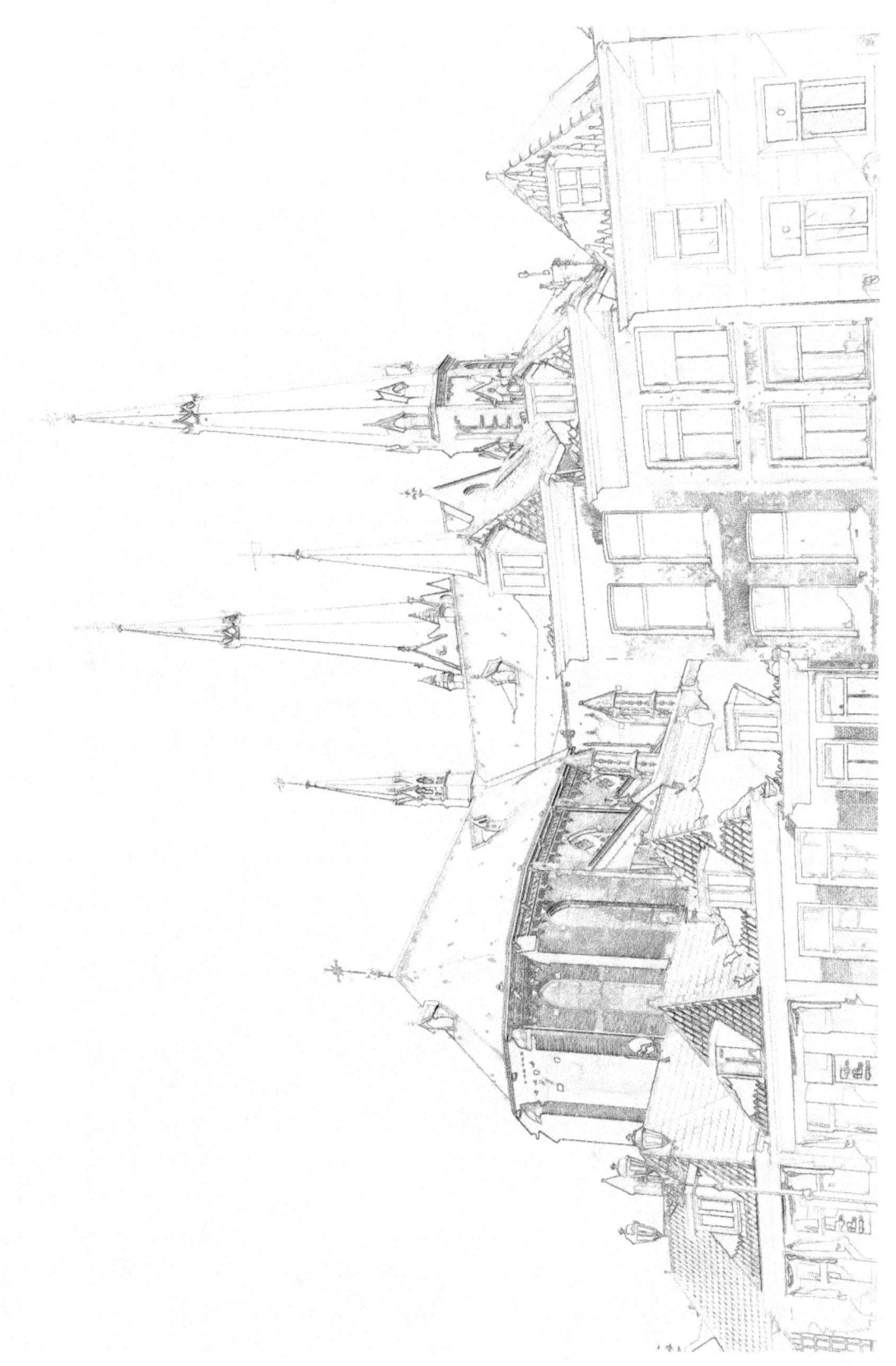

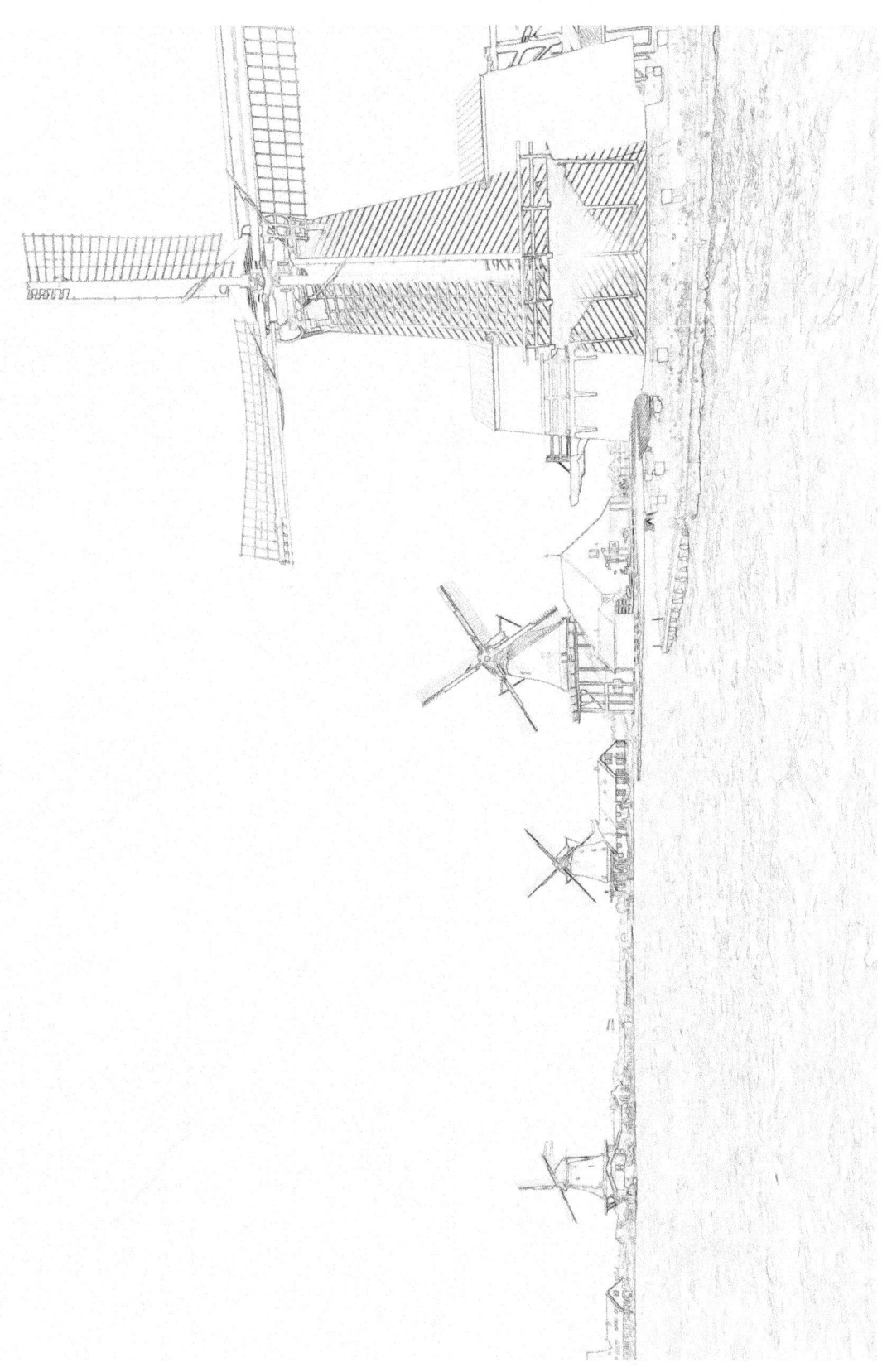

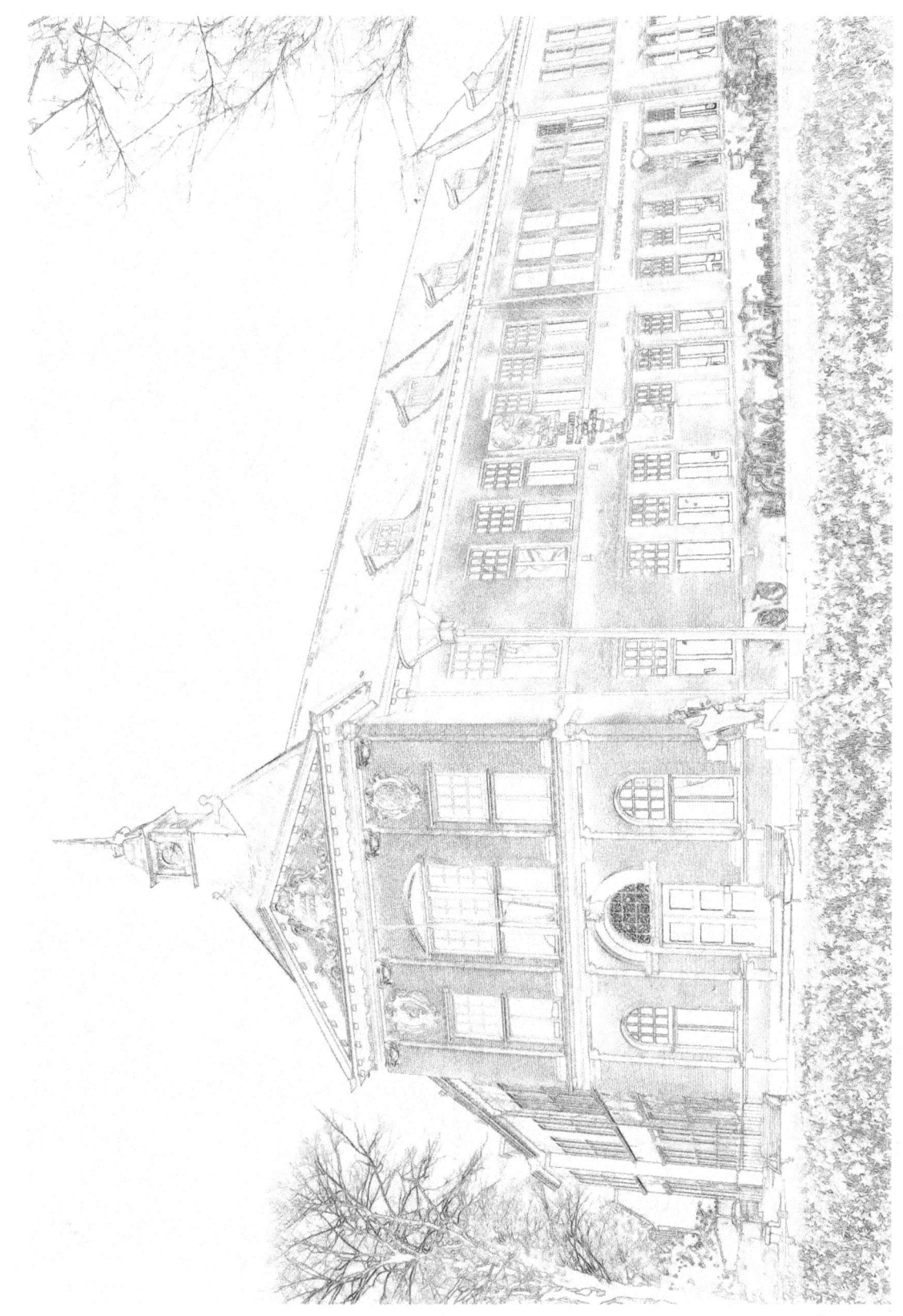

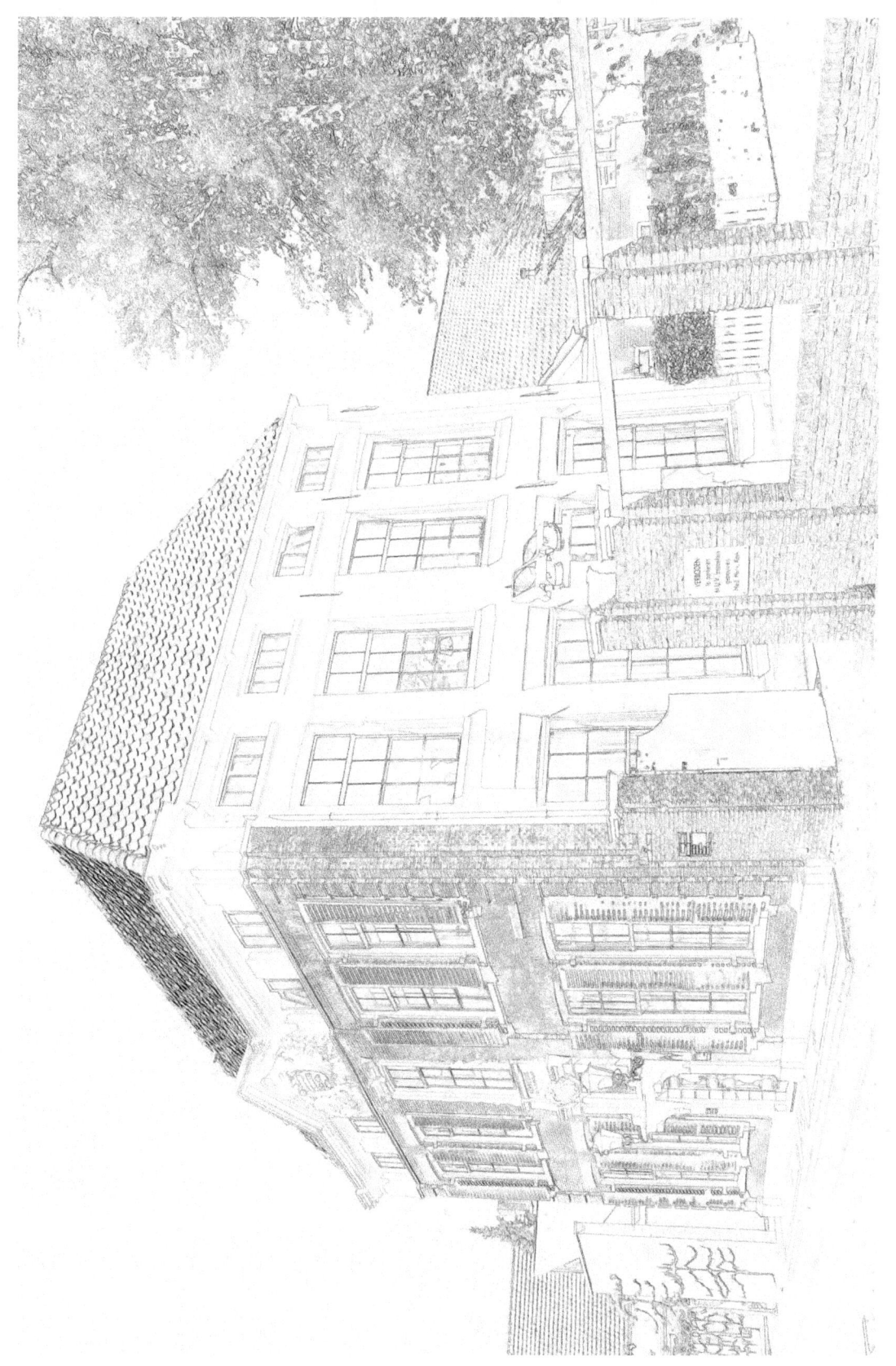

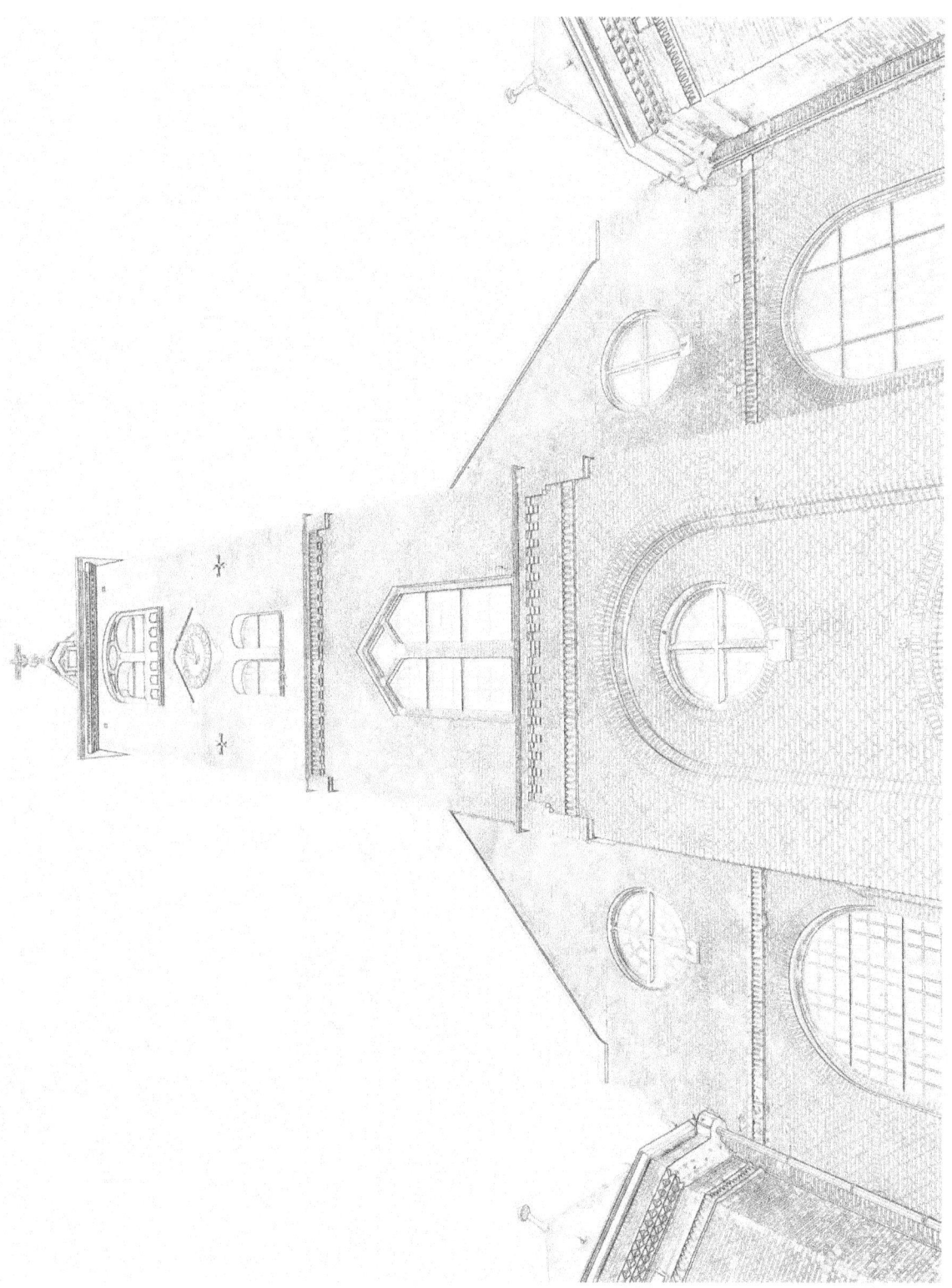

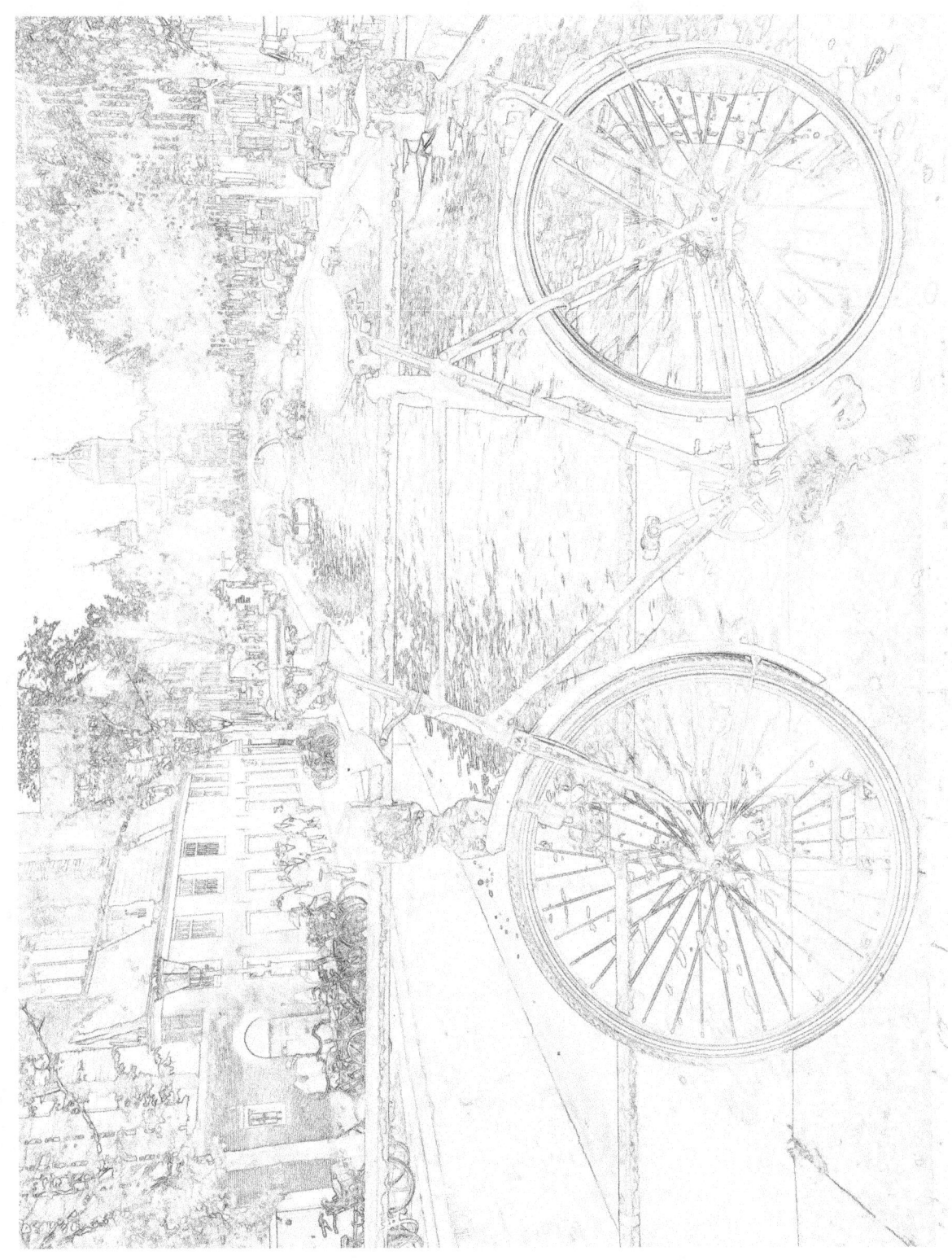

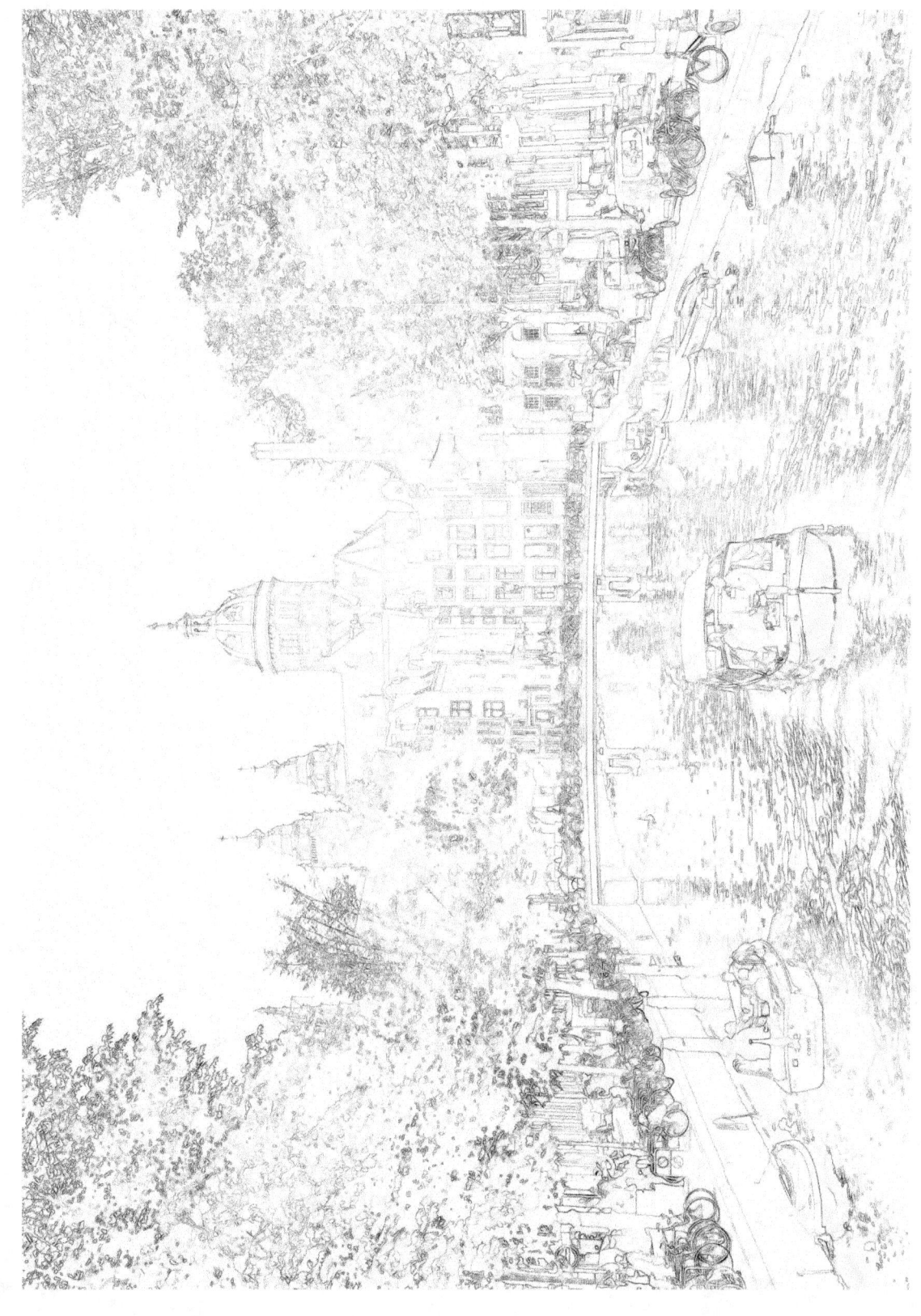

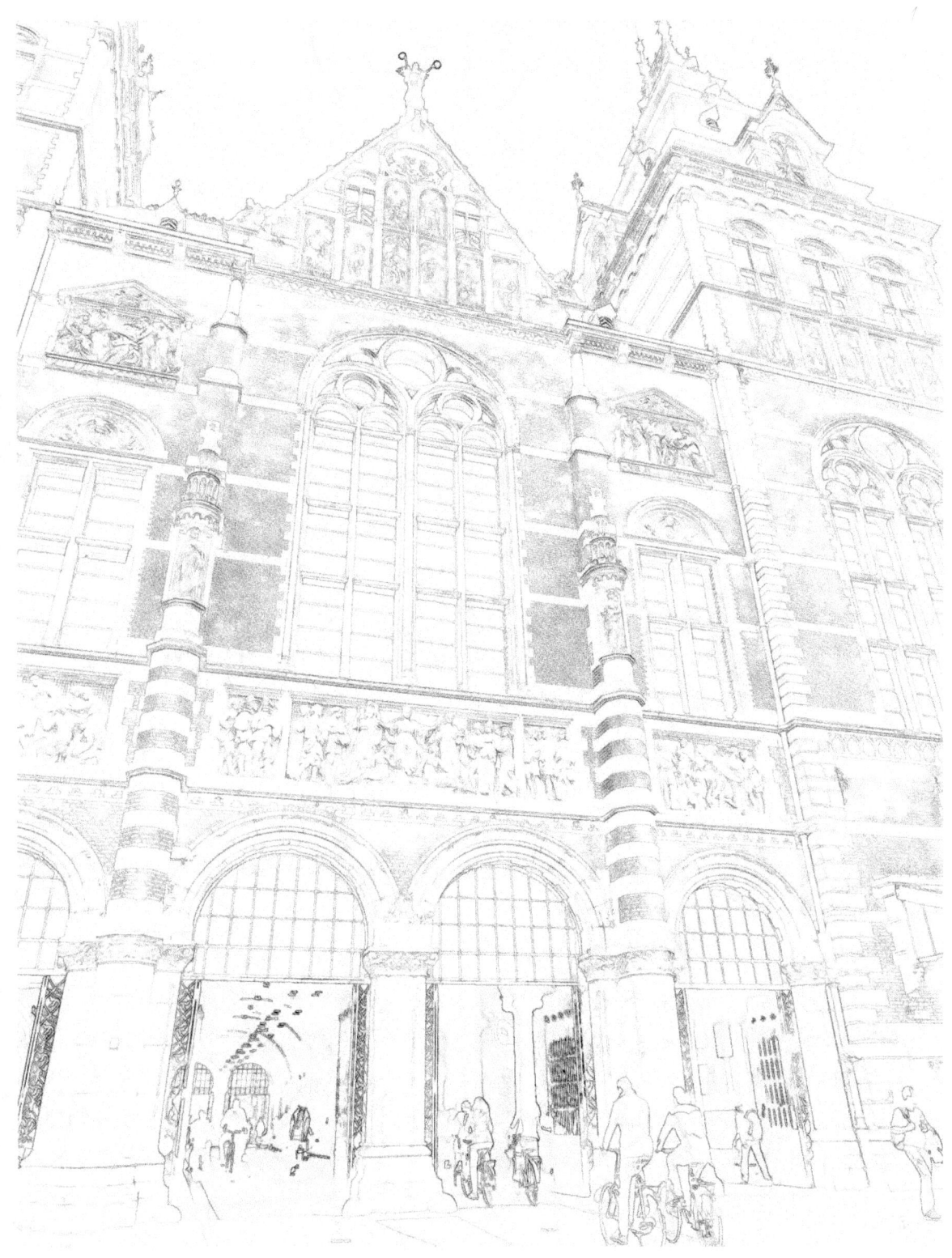

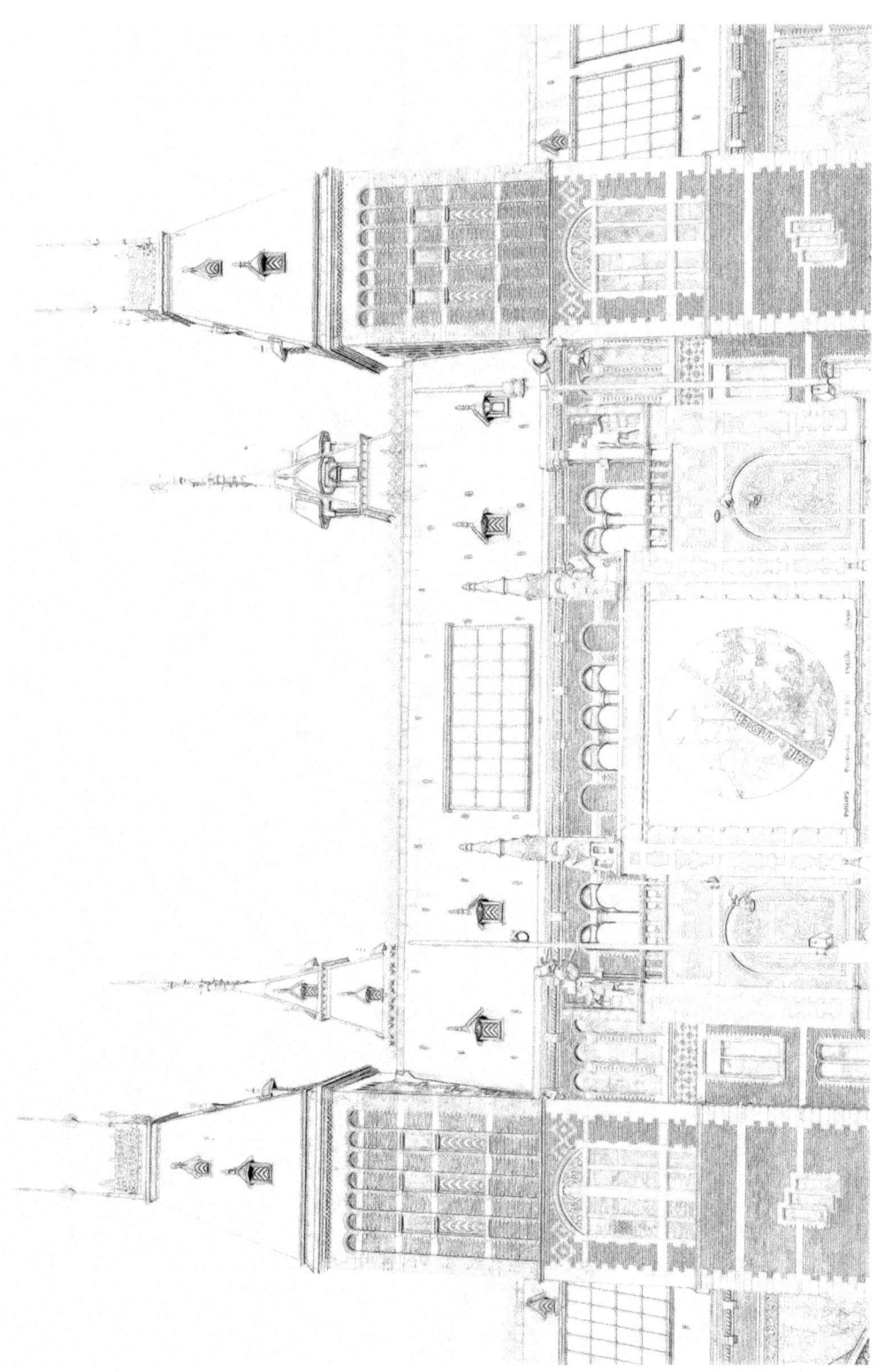

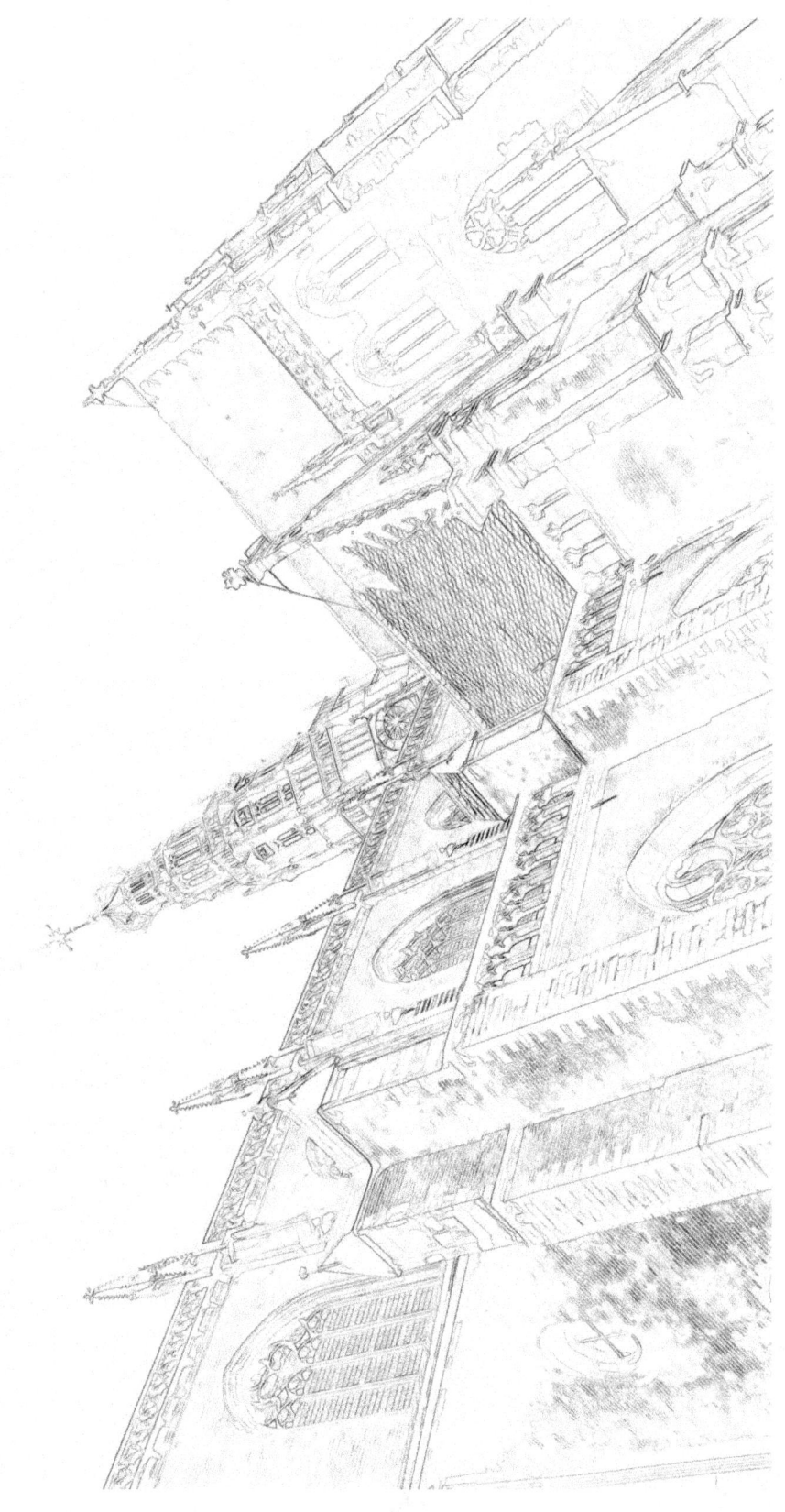

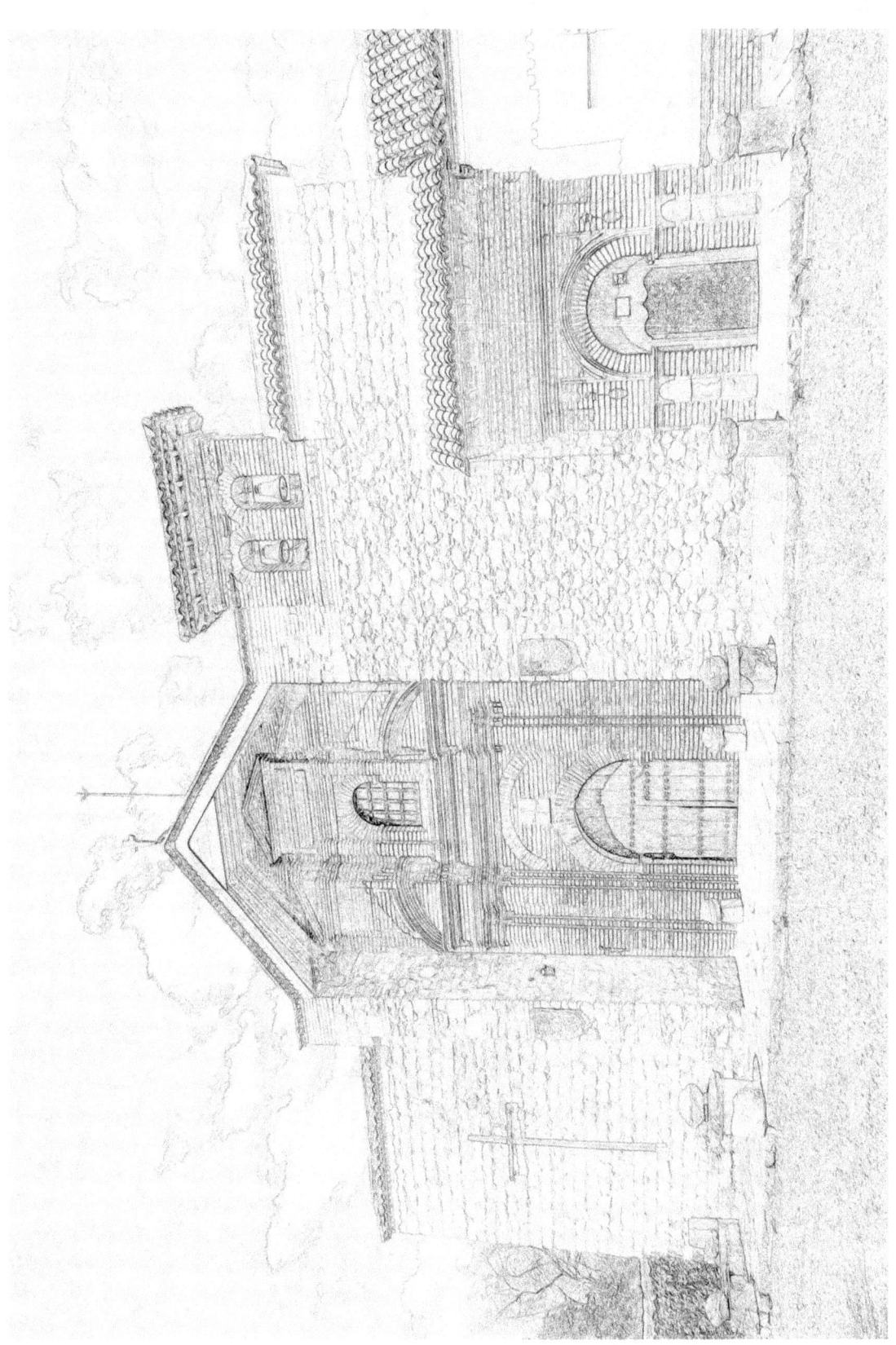

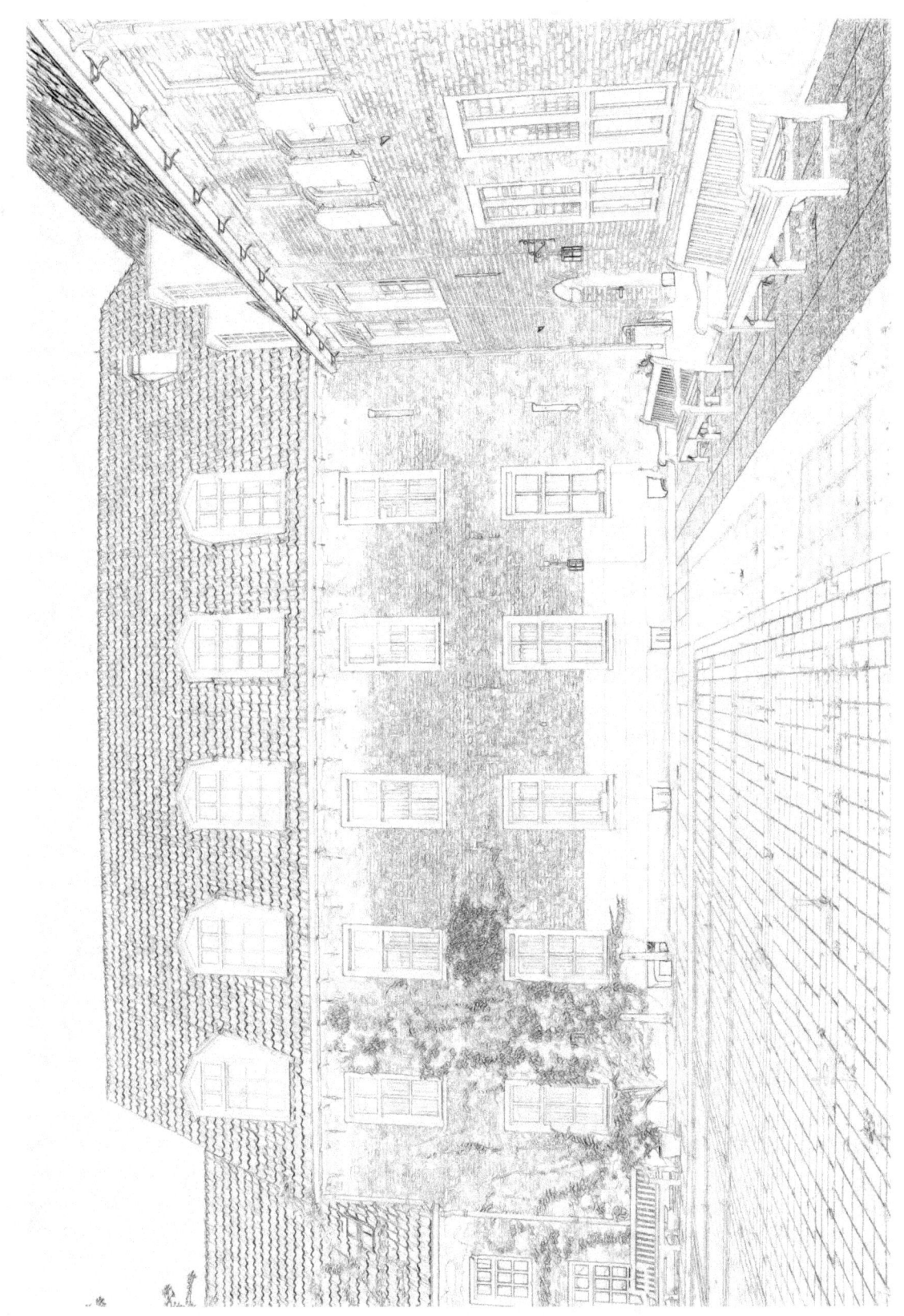

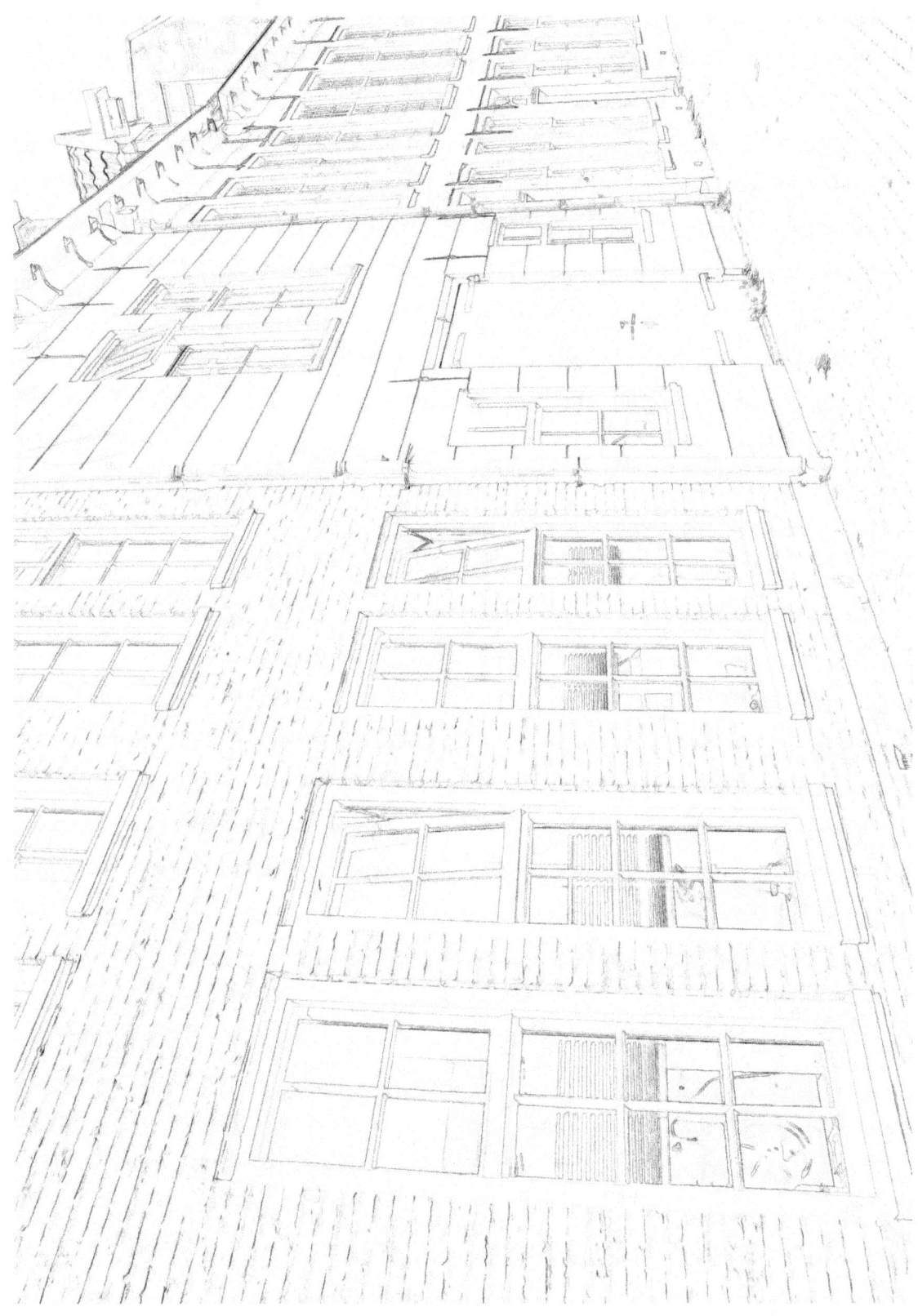

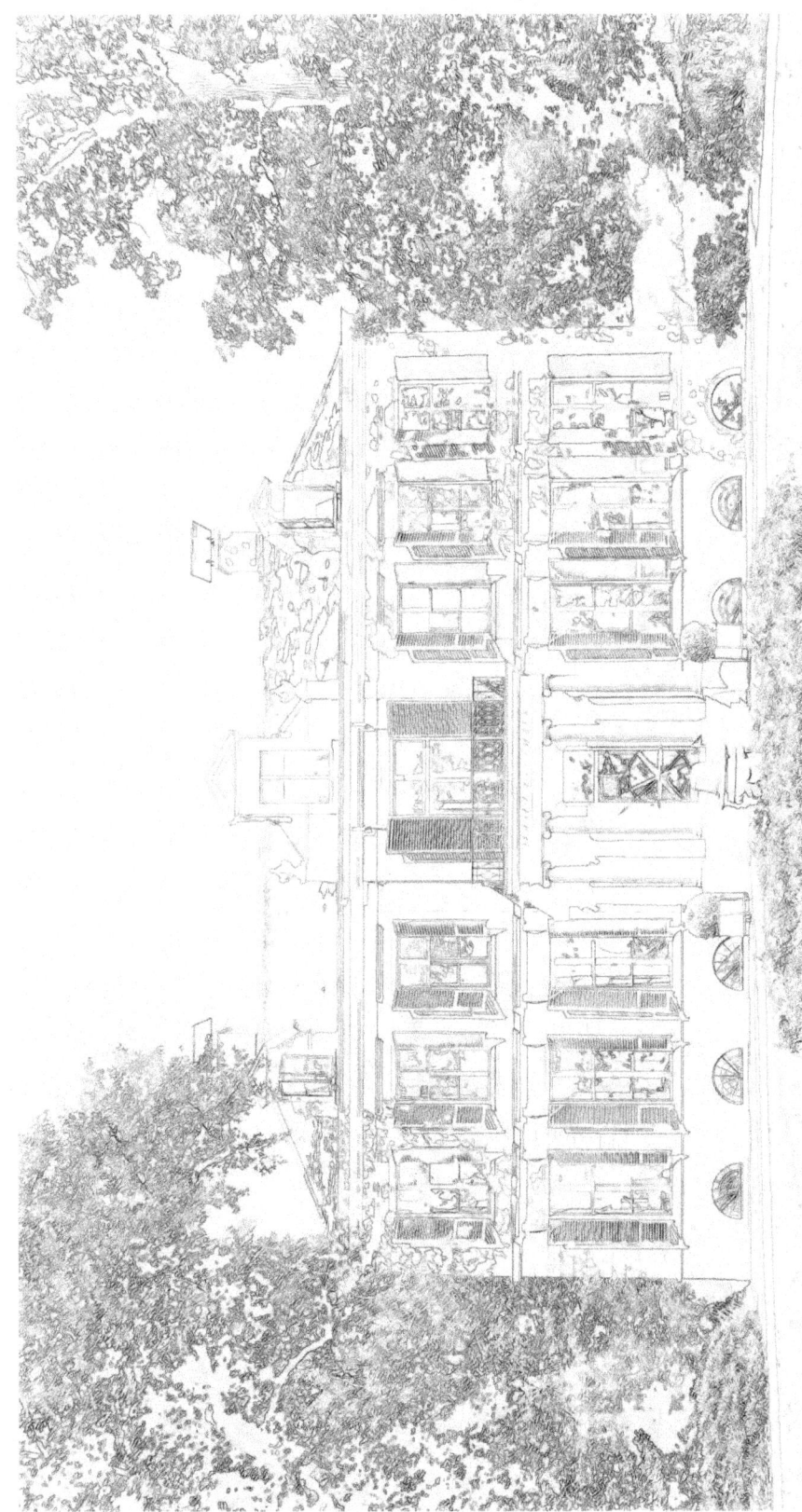

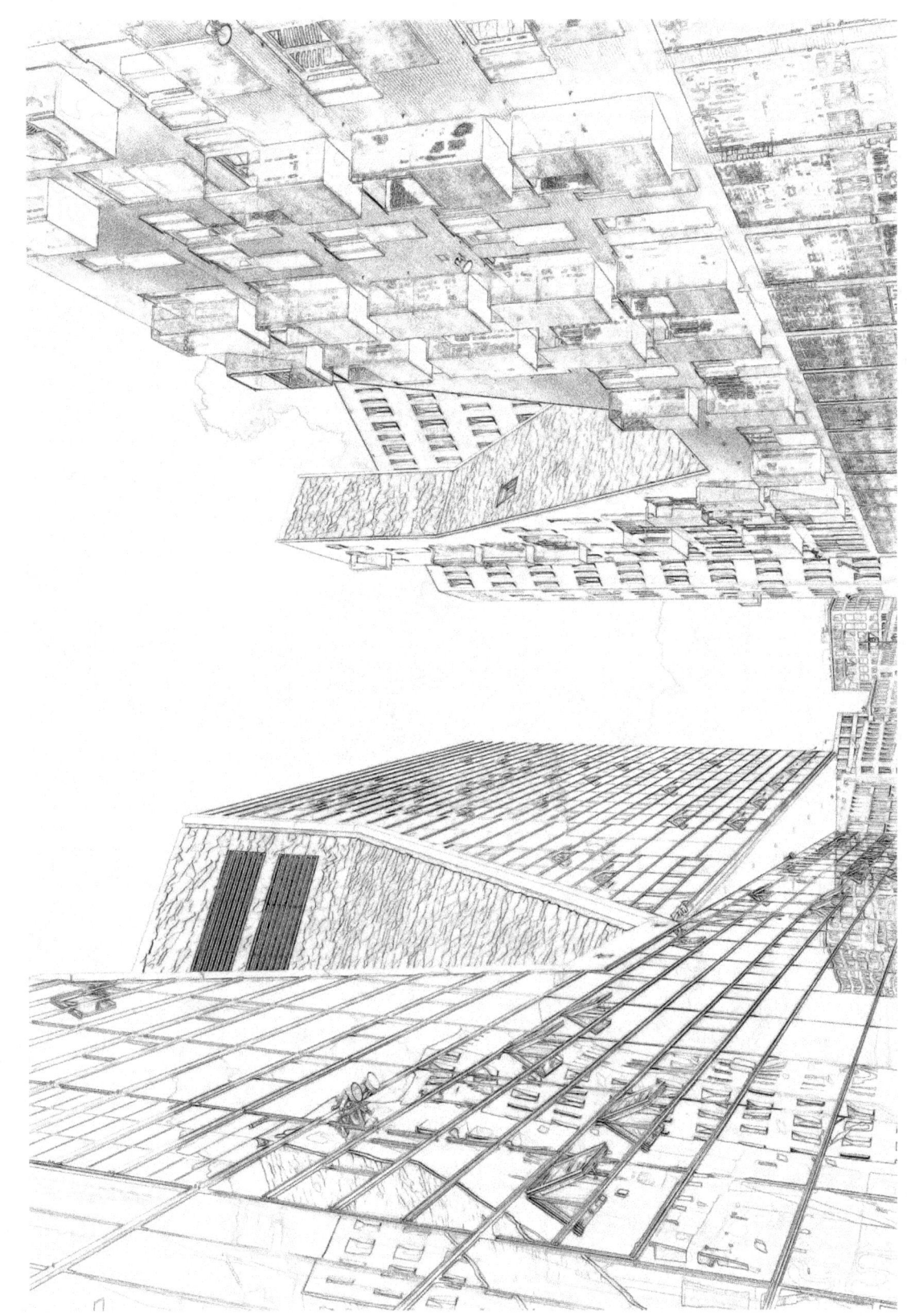

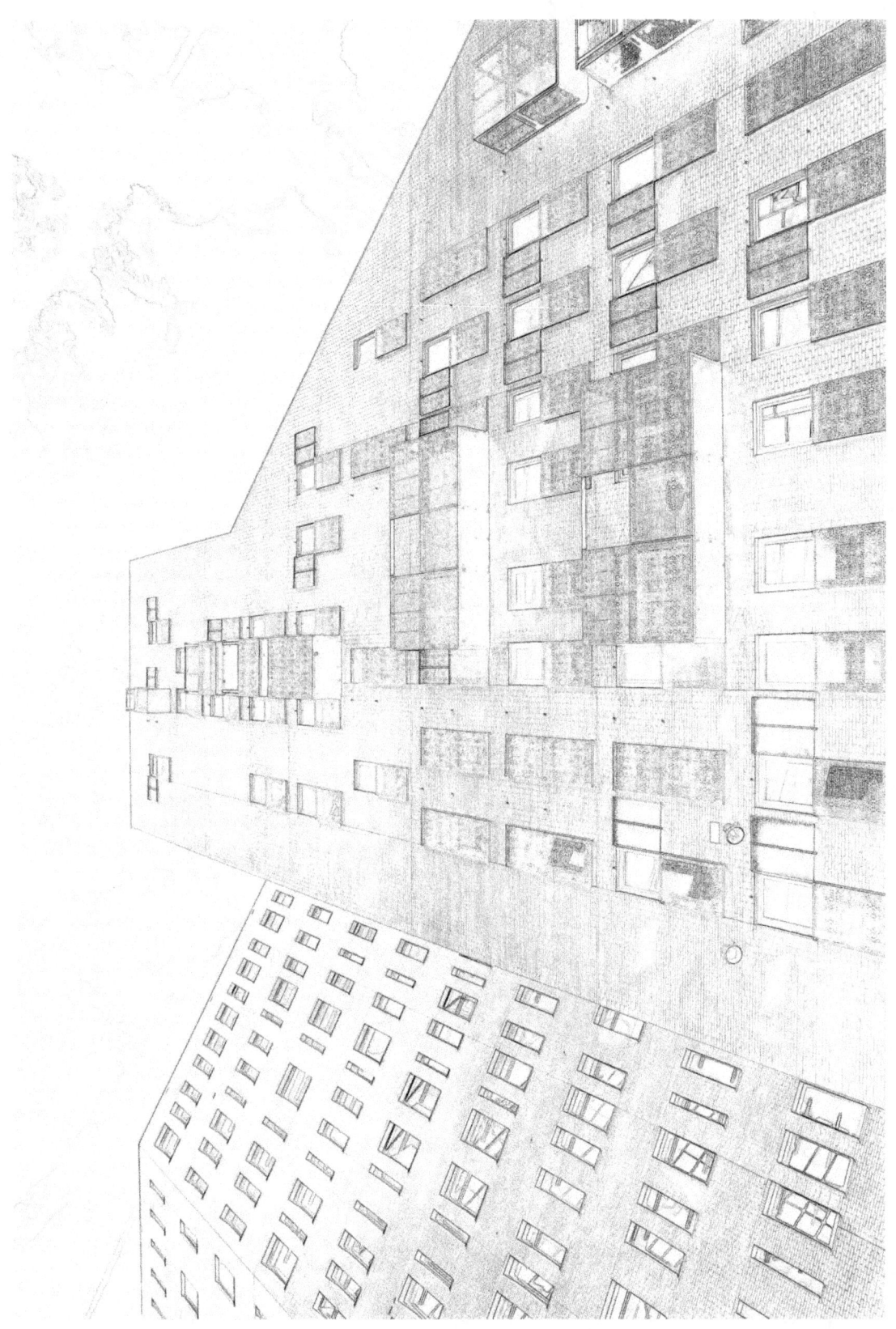

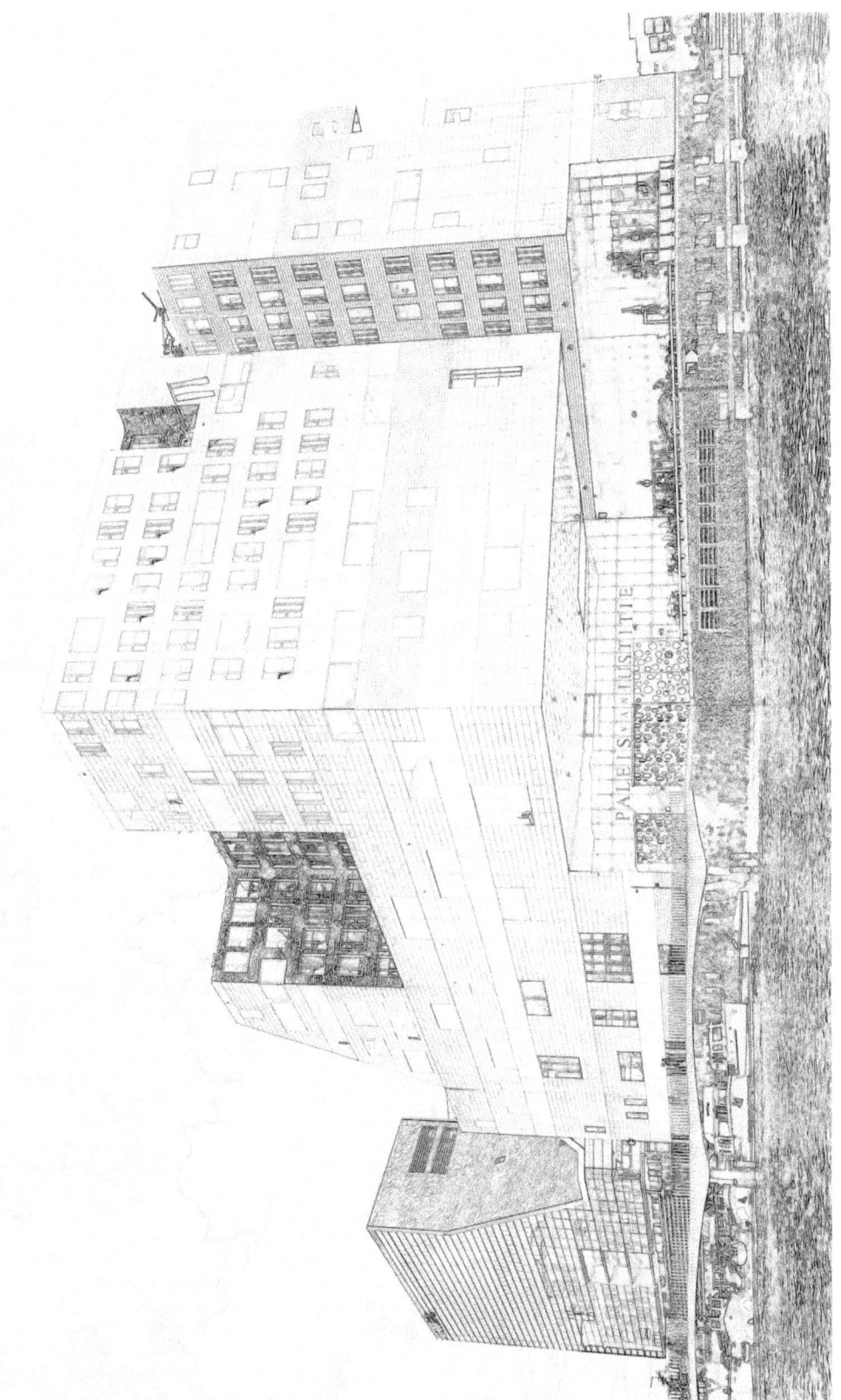

Picture Guide for this book : http://bit.ly/Netherland_Coloring

Don't Miss Another our Books.

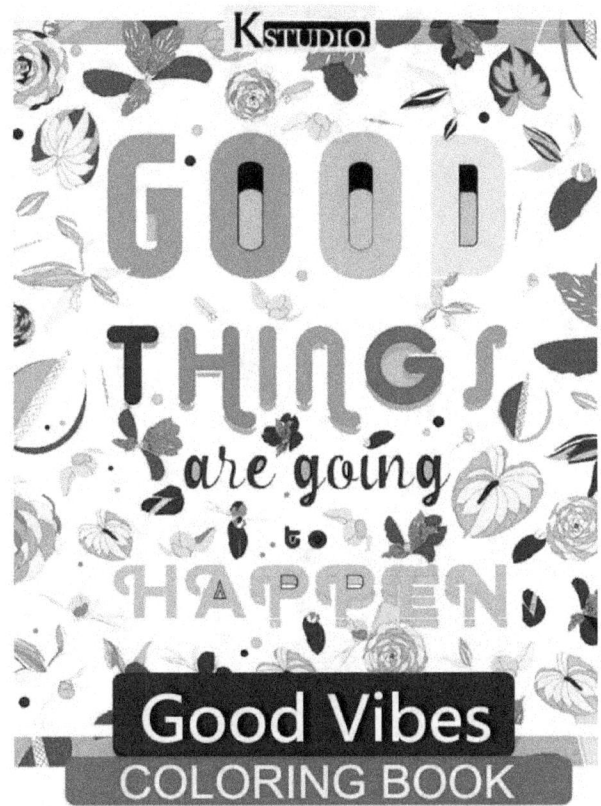

http://bit.ly/good_vibes_1

ISBN : 1530381223

(Use this ISBN for searching on amazon.com)

www.ingramcontent.com/pod-product-compliance
Lightning Source LLC
Chambersburg PA
CBHW081129180526
45170CB00008B/3057